KINGFISHER

First published 2010 by Kingfisher
an imprint of Macmillan Children's Books
a division of Macmillan Publishers Limited
20 New Wharf Road, London N1 9RR
Basingstoke and Oxford
Associated companies throughout the world
www.panmacmillan.com

Illustrated by Kath Grimshaw
Concept by Jo Connor

ISBN 978-0-7534-1957-1

Copyright © Macmillan Children's Books 2010

9 8 7 6 5 4 3 2 1
1TR/1209/TWP/UNT/150GSM/C

A CIP catalogue for this book is available
from the British Library.

Printed in China

WHAT'S IN THIS BOOK?

WHY...

HAVE YOU EVER ASKED YOURSELF WHY?

It's only natural to be confused by the world around us... It is a very complicated and surprising place sometimes! And you'll never understand what's going on around you unless you ask yourself 'WHY?' every now and again.

This is 'why' we have made this book.

We have travelled over the land, under the sea, up mountains, across deserts – and even into outer space – to collect as many tricky questions as we could find...

...and we also found the answers for you!

We now invite you to come with us on our journey around the world of 'WHY', so that we can show you all the answers we discovered.

Did you know...

Astronauts have to wear seatbelts to stop them floating away when they use the toilet. Space toilets do not flush. Everything is sucked away instead.

Astronauts on board a spacecraft can't feel gravity or see it working. Out in space, the Earth's gravity is not strong enough to hold them down, so they float about like balloons do.

WHY DO ASTRONAUTS FLOAT IN SPACE?

WHY IS EARTH SO SPECIAL?

Earth is the only planet in the Solar System with water and living things on it. This is because it is the third planet from the Sun, and it gets just the right amount of heat and light. Any closer, it would be too hot. Any further away and it would be too cold.

7

WHY DO STARS TWINKLE?

Stars twinkle only when we look at them from Earth. As starlight travels towards us, it is bent and wobbled by movement in the air surrounding Earth, so the stars look like they are twinkling.

Did you know...

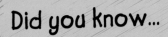

Sometimes flame-like sheets of glowing gas shoot out from a star. These are called prominences.

WHY DO DIVERS NEED HEADLIGHTS?

Sunlight only reaches down to 200 metres below the surface of the ocean. This 'sunlit zone' is where all sea plants and most sea animals live. From 1,000 metres onwards, it is totally dark.

WHY DO TREES HAVE LEAVES?

Trees need their leaves to stay alive. Leaves contain a sticky green stuff called chlorophyll. The chlorophyll uses water, sunlight and carbon dioxide in the air to make a sugary food. The food is then carried to every part of the tree in a sweet and gooey juice called sap.

Did you know...

In a single year, a forest of 400 trees gives off enough oxygen to keep at least 20 people breathing.

WHY DO LEAVES FALL IN THE AUTUMN?

Big green leaves make food while the Sun shines and the days are long. When the days get shorter, there is less time for making food and the tree must live off its food reserves. Rather than have to feed their leaves too, some trees shed their leaves in autumn.

Did you know...

Not all trees lose their leaves. Conifers have tough leaves that can withstand the winter cold.

WHY DO I FEEL DIZZY WHEN I SPIN AROUND?

In your ear, you have three loop-shaped tubes with liquid in them. This swishes about when you spin. Special nerves sense this movement and tell your brain you are spinning. If you stop suddenly, the liquid still swishes about for a bit. Your brain gets the wrong message and you feel dizzy!

WHY ARE EARS SUCH A FUNNY SHAPE?

The shape of your ears helps them to catch sounds from the air. The sounds go through your earhole into the hidden part, known as the inner ear, inside your head.

Did you know...

Ears have a drum in them. Your ear drum is a thin bit of skin, which vibrates when sounds hit it.

KEY

1. Ear drum
2. Tiny bones
3. Spiral tube
4. Nerves leading to brain

WHY DO CATERPILLARS CHANGE INTO BUTTERFLIES?

Every caterpillar has to go through four different stages of development before it becomes a fully-grown adult butterfly. At each stage, it changes its size, its shape and its colour.

Did you know...

Many kinds of insects change shape as they grow. This way of developing is called metamorphosis.

WHY DO TADPOLES GROW LEGS?

As they become older, tadpoles change into frogs. After a few weeks, they grow back legs, then front legs. Their tail and gills shrink back into their body and they develop lungs for breathing.

Did you know...

Adult mayflies live for just a few hours and try to find a mate before they die.

15

WHY DID CASTLES HAVE MOATS?

Did you know...

One way to beat enemies who shut themselves up in a castle was to surround it and wait for them to run out of food and water. This was called a siege.

Moats were deep, wide ditches filled with water, which surrounded a castle. They made it tricky for enemies to break into the castle. Friendly visitors could cross the moat over a drawbridge. But when enemies attacked, the drawbridge was raised.

WHY DID KNIGHTS WEAR ARMOUR?

In battle, knights were bashed and battered about by weapons such as swords and axes. They had to protect their bodies from all these sharp weapons, so they wore suits of tough metal armour.

Did you know...

Japanese knights were called samurai. Their armour was made of metal plates fixed to padded silk and leather.

WHY IS THERE A HOLE IN THE SKY?

High up in the atmosphere is the ozone layer, which absorbs most of the Sun's harmful rays. The ozone layer is damaged by chemicals called chlorofluorocarbons (CFCs for short), and a large hole has formed over Antarctica, letting in the damaging rays.

Did you know...

Jet aeroplanes fly in the ozone layer, between 10 and 40 kilometres above the Earth's surface. Their engines release chemicals that damage the layer.

WHY IS SUNLIGHT WARM?

Did you know...

Things that allow heat to pass through them easily are called conductors. Some metals are excellent conductors.

Sunlight is warm because the Sun gives off heat as well as light energy. The Sun's heat energy travels towards us in straight, invisible lines called heat rays. You cannot see them, but you can feel them on your skin on hot, sunny days.

WHY DO I GET ILL?

Did you know...

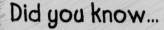 Some germs like dirt. Washing your body and cleaning your teeth help to keep these germs away.

Tiny germs and bacteria enter our bodies and can make us ill. Our body has the perfect temperature for these germs to grow and multiply. To help you get better, your immune system produces antibodies to fight the germs. By eating healthily and keeping fit, you can reduce the risk of getting ill.

20

WHY DO I CHATTER WHEN I'M COLD?

When you are cold, your muscles contract (become tighter) quickly to try and warm you up. This is called shivering. Your teeth chatter as the muscles in your jaw move.

WHY DO FLUTES HAVE HOLES?

To play the flute, you have to blow across the blowhole. The air shakes its way down the tube and you hear it come out as a musical sound. You change notes by covering and uncovering the different holes with your fingers.

Did you know...

A stringed instrument is tuned by turning the pegs at the end of its neck. Tightening a string makes a higher note, and loosening it makes a lower sound.

Did you know...

Air is invisible, so you cannot see the wind. But you can feel it on your face and see how it makes the trees sway.

WHY DOES THE WIND BLOW?

When you feel the wind blow, it's because air is moving. When the air is warm, it gets lighter and it rises up into the sky. Cooler air then rushes in to take its place, creating a breeze.

Did you know...

Even though they have poor eyesight, snakes can hunt in total darkness. They can sense the body heat of a nearby animal, and strike their prey with amazing accuracy.

As a snake's tongue darts in and out, it picks up scents in the air. The tongue carries these up to a sensitive area in the roof of the mouth, which 'tastes' the air. These sensors send messages to the brain, telling the snake whether a mate, a meal or an enemy is near.

24

Did you know...

Strong desert winds sometimes stir up huge clouds of sand. The wind-blown sand is powerful enough to strip the paint from a car.

WHY ARE DESERTS SANDY?

As the wind howls across land, it blasts against large rocks, and wears them away. Slowly, the rocks crack into stones and pebbles, which over time crumble into tiny sand grains.

WHY DO GIRAFFES HAVE LONG NECKS?

A giraffe's long neck makes it tall enough to eat the leaves at the top of trees. Other animals cannot reach as high, so the giraffe has lots to eat.

WHY CAN'T PENGUINS FLY?

Penguins cannot fly because their wings are too small to keep their heavy bodies up in the air. But penguins are very good swimmers and divers. They use their wings as paddles in the water.

Did you know...

The largest bird is the ostrich. It is too big to fly, but can run at twice the speed of the fastest Olympic runners.

WHY DO BIKES HAVE TYRES?

Tyres help a bike to grip the road safely. Look closely at a tyre and you will see that it is patterned. This pattern is called the tread. In wet weather, water escapes from under the tyre through grooves in the tread, stopping your bike from skidding.

Did you know...

As a rubber tyre rolls along, it rubs against the road. This rubbing creates a slowing force called friction, which helps the tyres grip.

Did you know...

Horseshoes have been used as good luck charms for hundreds of years.

Horseshoes help to stop hooves being damaged by hard surfaces such as roads. The shoes are usually made of steel, and the person who makes and fits them is called a farrier.

WHY DO HORSES WEAR SHOES?

Did you know...

The ostrich lays the heaviest eggs of any bird. Each one can weigh up to 1.3 kilograms – that's heavier than a bag of sugar.

WHY DO BIRDS LAY EGGS?

By laying babies inside eggs, a female bird can have several babies at once, and each one has a safe place in which to develop. When hatched, the babies can stay safely in the nest, while its parents fly off to find food.

Did you know...

A female crocodile carries her babies in her mouth, taking care not to bite them with her razor-sharp teeth.

A pouch is a safe place for a baby to grow. A new-born kangaroo is called a joey and is only the size of a peanut. It struggles through its mum's fur until it reaches her warm pouch. There, it feeds on her milk and carries on growing.

WHY CAN I SEE THROUGH GLASS?

Did you know...

The Moon reflects light from the Sun. It has no light of its own.

You can see through glass because it is transparent. This means it is almost clear, and it lets the light shine through. Glass is great for windows because it lets sunlight into a room and allows you to see what is happening outside.

WHY DO VOLCANOES BLOW THEIR TOPS?

Deep beneath an active, violent volcano is a vast chamber. Hot, runny rock and gases build up here until they blast upwards, under immense pressure, through cracks in the Earth's crust.

WHY ARE THERE NO DINOSAURS ON EARTH?

Did you know...

Many animals are 'endangered', meaning they are in danger of dying out, because people have hunted too many of them.

The dinosaurs lived on Earth for millions of years. Then, about 65 million years ago, they became extinct – every single one of them disappeared. No one really knows why, but one idea is that a massive meteorite hit the Earth and wiped them out.

WHY DO SPIDERS SPIN WEBS?

Spiders spin webs to catch food. When an insect flies into the web, it gets stuck. The spider rushes out to spin silk around it and the insect turns into a liquid mush. Later, the spider can suck it up, like a drink!

Did you know...

Many people think Tyrannosaurus could have run as fast as 50 kilometres an hour when chasing a meal.

WHY WAS TYRANNOSAURUS A BIG-MOUTH?

Tyrannosaurus was a huge meat-eater. At about six metres high, it stood three times taller than a grizzly bear. Its mouth was so big it could swallow a person whole!

Did you know...

The Romans invented concrete by mixing lime, water and ash from volcanoes. Concrete is as strong as stone and it sets hard, even under water.

WHY WERE ROMAN ROADS SO STRAIGHT?

The Romans were brilliant engineers. They used measuring instruments to work out where the road should go and chose the shortest, straightest route between two camps, forts or towns. The roads linked up the entire empire.

WHY WERE THE OLYMPICS HELD?

The Olympic Games were part of a religious festival in honour of Zeus, king of the gods. Every four years, thousands people flocked to Olympia – a place in ancient Greece – to watch athletes compete in games such as running, wrestling and racing chariots.

39

WHY DO HOT-AIR BALLOONS FLOAT?

The air inside a hot-air balloon is heated by a burner. When the air becomes warmer, it starts to rise as it is lighter than cold air. As the hot air rises, so does the balloon!

Did you know...

There are even taller mountains in space. Olympus Mons on the planet Mars is three times higher than Mount Everest, the tallest mountain on Earth.

WHY DO MOUNTAINS HAVE SNOW ON TOP?

Only the highest mountains have snow on top. When water gets very cold, it freezes and turns into snow or ice – and the higher you go up a mountain, the colder it gets.

WHY DO PLANTS HAVE FLOWERS?

Many plants have colourful, perfumed flowers that attract insects and other animals. When they feed on the sweet nectar inside the flower, they pick up a fine yellow dust called pollen, which they carry to another flower. When the pollen rubs off on the second flower, new seeds are made. This is called pollination.

Did you know...

The tiger is one of many animals that are in danger of dying out because their forest homes are being destroyed.

WHY DO WE CUT DOWN TREES?

Throughout history, people have cut down trees for their wood. Forests are also destroyed to clear land for farming, and to build towns and cities.

WHY DO LEOPARDS HAVE SPOTS?

A leopard's spots help it to hide among the trees and bushes so it can jump out and surprise its prey. The light and dark markings in its fur match the patches of sunlight and shadow under the leafy branches.

Did you know...

Mosquitoes are attracted to humans by their smell. They particularly like the scent of hot, sweaty feet!

WHY DO SKUNKS STINK?

If a skunk feels threatened by a predator, it sprays a stinking, sticky fluid at its attacker's eyes. The liquid smells so badly, it can make the predator sick, allowing the skunk to escape.

WHY ARE OCTOPUSES LIKE JET PLANES?

Octopuses, squid, cuttlefish and scallops all use jet propulsion to move. Octopuses pump water in over their gills and squirt it out through a fleshy tube called a siphon. They steer by pointing the siphon in different directions.

Did you know...

Some types of fish can 'walk'. Batfish have a pair of long, thick fins underneath their body. They use these to creep over the bottom of the ocean.

WHY DO WHALES SING?

Whales are talkative animals. They bellow, grunt, yelp and make bubbling noises to find other whales and send messages. Male humpback whales sing long tunes, sometimes repeating them for hours or days. This is probably to attract a mate.

Did you know...

Each bird has its own special song. Birds recognize each other by their songs, just as humans recognize friends by their voices.

WHY DOES THE SUN RISE?

Did you know...

The ancient Greeks believed that the Sun was a god called Helios, and that he rode across the sky in a chariot of flames.

The Sun does not really rise at all! It is the Earth that turns around to give you a sunrise each morning. Wherever you are, it starts to get light as your part of the Earth moves round to face the Sun.

WHY DO ANIMALS SLEEP IN WINTER?

Did you know...

Many animals grow thick coats in winter to help them survive the bitter cold.

For some animals, sleeping is the best way to survive the hungry winter days. Chipmunks, squirrels, hedgehogs and some bears eat as much as they can in the autumn, then hibernate (sleep) somewhere safe until springtime.

WHY IS THE SEA SALTY?

Sea water tastes salty because it has salt in it! The same kind of salt is used on food. Most of it comes from rocks on the land. Rain washes the salt into rivers, which carry it to the sea.

Did you know...

It is easier to float in salty sea water than it is in fresh water. The Dead Sea in the Middle East is the world's saltiest sea – swimmers cannot sink in it, even without armbands!

WHY DO ARMBANDS HELP ME FLOAT?

When you blow up your armbands, you are putting lots of air inside them. Air is much lighter than water, so it helps you to float.

WHY DO BRIDGES SWAY?

Did you know...

If army ants have to cross gaps, some of them join up to make a bridge for the others to crawl over.

Bridges can bend and sway about as much as two or three metres. If bridges were completely stiff and rigid, a very strong wind might crack them.

WHY DO SHIPS FLOAT?

Did you know...

Humans blink every two to ten seconds, and each blink takes about 0.3 seconds. This means that you spend about 30 minutes every day with your eyes shut.

WHY DO GLASSES HELP YOU FOCUS?

When things are put into water, they make room for themselves by pushing it aside. Although ships are heavy, they are hollow and have high sides. This means they can settle quite low in the water, pushing a lot of it aside. In fact, a ship won't sink unless it is overloaded and becomes more dense than the water it pushes aside.

If you are short-sighted, far away objects are less clear. If you are long-sighted, near objects may seem blurry. People are long or short-sighted because the lenses in their eyes are not quite the right shape. So they wear glasses or contact lenses to help them see more clearly.

QUICK-QUIZ QUESTIONS

1. What 'g' holds you to the ground?

2. Earth is the third planet from the Sun. True or false?

3. What are prominences?

4. How far underwater can humans dive?

5. What does chlorophyll use to make food for trees?

6. Conifer trees lose their leaves in winter. True or false?

7. What is metamorphosis?

8. Unscramble RED BIRD WAG to show what castles use to keep enemies out.

9. Where did samurai knights come from?

10. Aeroplanes are good for the environment. True or false?

11. What helps to fight germs in your body?

12. Which is lighter – warm or cold air?

13. Snakes have very good eyesight. True or false?

14. What is the biggest bird on Earth?

15. Unscramble COIN RIFT to show what force helps tyres to grip.

16. What is a baby kangaroo called?

17. When did the dinosaurs die out?

18. Who invented cement to be used in building roads?

19. Who was king of the gods in ancient Greek stories?

20. Where did the first hot-air balloon ride take place?

21. What is the tallest mountain on Earth?

22. What is pollination?

23. How much of the Earth's water is salty?

24. Which sea is the saltiest?

25. Unscramble BE IN EARTH to show what some animals do in winter.

QUICK-QUIZ
ANSWERS

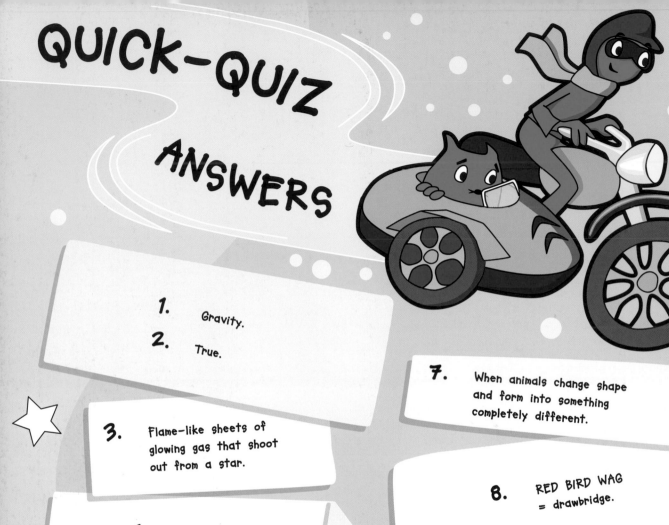

1. Gravity.
2. True.
3. Flame-like sheets of glowing gas that shoot out from a star.
4. 200 metres.
5. Sunlight, water and carbon dioxide.
6. False. Conifer leaves can withstand the cold winter.
7. When animals change shape and form into something completely different.
8. RED BIRD WAG = drawbridge.
9. Japan.
10. False. They release chemicals that damage the Earth's atmosphere.
11. Antibodies produced by the immune system.

12. Warm air.

13. False. Snakes have very poor eyesight.

14. The ostrich.

15. COIN RIFT = friction.

16. A joey.

17. About 65 million years ago.

18. The Romany.

19. Zeus.

20. Paris, France, in 1783.

21. Mount Everest.

22. When grains of pollen are carried from one flower to another so that new seeds can be made.

23. About 97%

24. The Dead Sea

25. BE IN EARTH = hibernate (sleep through a cold winter).

TRICKY WORDS

BACTERIA
Germs that can cause illness and infections.

CARBON DIOXIDE
A colourless, invisible gas that animals exhale (breathe out).

CHARIOT
An ancient, horse-drawn vehicle.

ABSORB
To soak up or take in.

ANTARCTICA
Earth's icy, southernmost area around the South Pole.

ANTIBODIES
Tiny parts of the body created by the immune system to find and fight germs and keep the body free from illness.

ARMOUR
A covering that protects a body from harm.

ASTRONAUT
A person who travels into space to find out more about it.

ATMOSPHERE
The layer of gases surrounding a planet. Earth's atmosphere keeps in the heat from the Sun, but also keeps out many harmful rays from the Sun.

EARTH'S CRUST
The outer layer of planet Earth, on which we live.

EMPIRE
A large area of land, usually several countries, ruled by one government. The Romans had a huge empire.

EXTINCT
When not one of a type of animal or plant is alive.

FORT
A building like a castle that contains armed soldiers.

GAS
Something that isn't solid or liquid. Oxygen is a gas.

GERMS
Tiny living things that can cause illness.

GILLS
The breathing parts on an underwater creature. Water is breathed through gills, which take out the oxygen in the water so that the creature can breathe.

GRAVITY
A force of attraction between objects. This happens in space, for example, where a moon is held in orbit around a planet, because the planet is more massive.

IMMUNE SYSTEM
The body's system that fights harmful germs by creating antibodies.

JET PROPULSION
When something moves by squirting a rush of water behind it, which pushes it forwards.

LUNGS
The organs in the body that help creatures breathe by supplying the body with oxygen.

METEORITE
A rock from space that falls down to Earth.

MULTIPLY
To increase in number.

NERVES
Parts inside the body that sense pain.

ORBIT
The path of an object as it travels around something. The Earth orbits the Sun.

OXYGEN
A colourless, invisible gas in air that animals need to breathe in order to live.

PREDATOR
An animal that hunts and eats another animal.

PREY
An animal that is hunted and eaten by another animal.

REFLECT
To bend back light from a surface. A mirror bends back light so you can see your reflection.

ROMAN
Of an ancient people from Italy who lived around 2,000 years ago in Europe, Africa and Asia.

SCENT
A smell.

SENSITIVE
Being able to react to one or several of the five senses of touch, taste, smell, sight or hearing.

SENSOR
A part of an animal's body that detects things for a particular sense, such as taste or smell.

SILK
Fine threads that are made by insects and woven together to make a soft, smooth and strong material.

SOLAR SYSTEM
The Sun and the objects in space that orbit it, including the eight planets.

STEEL
A strong metal.

TRANSPARENT
Something that is clear or see-through.

VIBRATE
To move back and forth quickly.

WHERE TO FIND STUFF

Wow! What an amazing journey! We hope you had as much fun as we did, and learnt many new things. Who knew there was so much to discover about 'why'! Speaking of 'who', we can tell you that we'll soon be going on a few more exciting journeys:

The Book Of... How?
The Book Of... What?
The Book Of... Who?

Look out for these great books! 'Who' knows 'what' we'll discover...

See you soon!